THE ENIGMA

M N BATHRU NISHA . A DEEPTI CELLINA . M F SANOFER BURVEEN

Contents

Contents

Preface

"The Enigma" (Unravel the Truth) is co-authored by three budding writers, M.N.Bathru Nisha, A. Deepti Celina, M.F. Sanofer Burveen, The three different author's over pours a great amount of innocuous feelings with the urge to soothe the readers heart. It is done with the sincere contribution by all the three writers and with their constant hard work. It acts as a great antidote and discusses various levels of emotions that reflects a common layman's day to day life. Let's see what two our authors have to say to their readers,

"I feel so blessed to finally publish my second book next to "The Unalloyed Solicitude". It's an great honour and pleasure to co-author this book along with my other two friends. My poems which comes under the title, "A Cry in the Wilderness" describes the dark side of human emotions and also provides the remedy to overcome them. These poems are done with conscious effort and hope to get your support more in my future endeavors.

- M.N. Bathru Nisha"

"I'm beyond thankful to God for having bestowed me with an opportunity to co-author this book . My part in this book titled under "The Memories of Little Wounds" will be shedding light on raw emotions, that I've dealt with and carried within me for so long.

These are the words that I've Longed to shout out aloud but never had a chance or found the right time to convey them. Be it , my feelings, my agitation, my insecurities, I've tried to capture everything as authentic as I can, for the readers to cherish and reflect on . I'll stop with this and let you read the rest. Hope my words speak for themselves! Touchwood! with any luck, I believe, you'll find this book gratifying and pleasurable, as it for us!

~ M.F. Sanofer Burveen ”

Authors Note

Meet, **Ms. A. DEEPTI CELLINA** One of our key authors and has contributed around eight poems titled under **PARTIALITY PHILTRE**, She is a literature enthusiast and is currently doing her B.Ed Programme in St. John's College of Education, a reputed institude in Tirunelveli. Having completed her UG degree in English Literature, She is also doing her Masters as well, via correspondence. She has been a part of many co-authored books, some of which are ***Niharika, Confessions, It's Her Choice*** and ***Modern Mind.***

Meet, **Ms. M N BATHRU NISHA,** an English Literature student, who is currently doing her Master's in English. She had published her own book titled **"AN UNALLOYED SOLICITUDE"**, a collection of ten poems. She is passionate about her love for litera ture, for which she opted her mainstream studies as English. She is a great orator, who has won several awards in many inter-collegiate competitions. She is also a part-time content writer. It was a great pleasure to have her on board and she has contributed around Ten poems for THE ENIGMA under the title **A CRY IN THE WILDERNESS**.

Meet our talented compiler and one of our co-authors, **Ms. M.F. SANOFER BURVEEN**, A writer and a literature enthusiast, She has contributed immensely for this project by her writings. In THE ENIGMA, which is her second work, She has come up with around eleven poems, presented under the title **THE MEMORIES OF LITTLE WOUNDS**, She is currently pursuing her Masters in English. She's also a budding blogger and a part time content writer. She had previously published her first work named **THE ANECDOTES.**

Authors Note

A CRY IN THE WILDERNESS

1. THE EMPTY ME

There are many things hidden inside of me,
It made me change a lot.
It weakened me and binds my hands,
It locked me in a dark room.
The pieces of lost time,
The memories of love that threw away,
They have been deleted and abandoned
Only shells remain.
The agony that I felt deep inside of my veins,
Got me struck in my past.
Can't able to get out of it
Trapped in a beautiful lie,
Of this undutiful world.
Sweetened lies of truth,
Changed me drastically,
Into a different human,
That I was not even aware of.
Thought this would just be a sway,
But it just thought to stay.
Snatched away the real me
Running behind the time,
That is trying to seize away something from me.
It leaves an empty vacant hole inside me,
A sense of lavishness blinded my eyes ,
The feeling of getting blown apart into pieces.

The tears that turns into precious rubies as they drop,
Was not aware of its worth.
A mere existence I felt,
Caresses my cheek, brushes through my hair.
Wished to catch hold of it,
But it escaped before I could make any further attempt.
Wishing to claim it, one or the other day, that can rescue me from the pitch dark of this world,
But it leaves behind the empty me!!

2. SAFE IN DAD'S ARMS

Deep through my veins,
Your love runs through
A frantic love,
That never douse.
My fears made your tears
Reckless of the problems you faced,
You were my only dear!
You were my PAPA,
P stands for Protector,
A stands for Affectionate,
And the last two words,
Which I hail you by, Pa!
You are my knight shining in armour,
Who shields me,
From the fantasy of the murky world.
I inhibit your thoughts,
Which I exhibit through my feelings.
Your subjection,
gets my objection.
But your liveliness brings back my gleefulness.
You, who care for me,
Taking care of my footwear,
Conscious to an extent,
That my feet should not lie low.
I humbly bow my head to your low!!!

3. MY TREASURER

When my nightmares chase me towards darkness,
You were there as my savior.
My mightiest one,
Who sustained my arrogance,
And tolerated my insults.
We were known as siblings,
But you are more like an archangel to me.
You dashed my inner veil,
And let me in,
In the world full of monsters.
You heartened me to fight against these demons.
Your innocuous nature tended my weak heart
You made my shortcomings to turn,
As my upcomings in my dreadful life.
When I pester you with so many troubles as an input,
You showed me your immense love as an output.
Though my love for you is not upto the core,
My selfishness of you, belonging to me,
Shall never fade!

4. THE SO CALLED "UNTOUCHABLES"

It was God, who painted all of us,
With different colours.
It was him, who created each and everyone differently,
So that each one can be recognised individually.
Even now, people reckon that, the Whites are higher-calibre,
And the Blacks are unworthy.
They are even considered as "THE UNTOUCHABLES"
Our eyeballs are made up of the colour,Black.
Even if it's lost,
Our whole World will look dark,
And not bright.
It's a matter of fact,
That, our skin is the largest organ in our body.
But, it is the only fragile organ, which can be ripped off very easily.
Even our life is not as bright as always
We are indeed, enforced to walk through the dark paths,
In order to reach the bright destination.
Black stands for power, independent, strong-will and determination.
And who are we to look down upon the Blacks,
When our hearts are filled with full of black soot and filthy thoughts?
Our skin will get bruises in grey or Black, when we get hurt,
And not in white.
There are millions of people, who are in between the two extremes,
In perfect blends.

Then, why it was only him, who was suffocated to death, even when he didn't commit any crime?
Our skin may be contrasting,
But, we all are fabricated by the same elements as humans.
Does the colour Black matters a lot,
Even when the whole humanity is yet to die?

5. HIT BY THE SEASON OF SADNESS

My wings of freedom is clipped,
I am jailed inside a veil,
A veil of darkness,
With ruptured tinch of regret and fear.
Tormented to the most
Torn apart by the mist of sadness,
Gleaming up towards me,
Fought hard to cleave apart,
But found myself clinged onto it.
Weather of sadness and a season of folly,
Made my immature self to return back,
Dashed upon the conscience of my mind,
Leaving behind my wisdom.
Wished to climb great hills,
But got greater chills.
Leaned onto my burdens,
Which overtook my load of happiness.
Fought to survive long,
Every now and then
Still had many speculating thoughts running on my mind,
Wished to stop fantasizing the world of my own,
And created an empty visionary of my throne

6. THE HOLY MONTH

A very familiar one, who comes once in a year,
Stood infront of my doorsteps,
And anticipated for the right hour to invade my home.
In the fullness of time, when the thin slice of the crescent moon appeared,
It set foot in my house,
Retrieved my life from darkness to luminescence.
It is called to mind as a holy month,
Elevated me to plunge into my ethical verge to the fullest.
A blessed month is casting it's shadow upon me.
The twilight became more sublime than day,
Long-standing night prayers, better than the thousand months,
Wasn't no longer gruelling my tootsie and it was a boon,
Made my heart to soothe in a state of tranquility.
It fed my soul.
It made me to perceive the divine side of me,
Initiated in me, the fervour to recite the Holy Book more.
It made my time innumerable,
As I diligently engaged myself invoking to my Lord.
I eschewed my sustenance,
And fasted the whole day, gratifying my Lord, from dawn till dusk.
For Him my breath is the fragrance of musk.
My mouth always babbles reciting the Holy words.
The Muslims, who pray and fast with zest,
Are aware of the rewards, of this month's manifest.

Throughout this month, I weep and repent,
Now is the time to strongly lament
And those who shun this sacred month,
In the Day of Reckoning will face the brunt.
In the last ten night's, hides the Night of Decree,
I plea to God for benevolence.
The Angels descends with Gabriel in the lead,
To check on the steadfast and record of my every deed.
This month embroiled the night's of power.
The Zakah I remunerated,
Gets added to my deeds.
It's a unique month and has no twin.
In this month, there is something habitual, Which is forming accurately every ritual.
The month to ask forbearance for my sins;
The month, where the Devil's are chained and the Gates of Paradise is wide unlatch.
The aroma of Heaven gets to the core of my soul,
And urges me more to be conscientious towards my Lord.
But, these momentous events supervene, only in the Holy month of Ramadan,
Where Allah's blessings, wholly descends upon his mankind.
And let's not squander this pivotal and celestial Ramadan, merely just by enduring thirst and hunger, throughout the day.
Rather let's remember and exalt our Lord,
And let's do infinite quantum of good deeds,
with an eye towards a place in Jannah

7. REMEMBER

When the nights are drawn out,
And days absconds swiftly,
Remember! Life is now going to be a arduous one.
When people finds fault with you,
Denounce you brazenly,
Gives varying remarks about your attire,
Remember! Life is now a game-changer.
When the fantasy world starts to diminish,
And the real world takes out it veil,
Remember! Life is like sailing on the middle of a sea.
When the whole world dwindles,
When the nightmare conjures your heart,
Remember! Life is a catastrophe.
When the silver line of the blue sky starts to fade,
And the images of the cloud are not captivating as it was before,
Remember! Life can get tangled up.
When solitary strikes you the most,
Only the memories can accompany you.
Remember! Life is a battlefield,
Battling for the life is the main goal to achieve
And if you fail,
You shall never get the bail.

8. A WARRIOR

Agitated by my fears,
Embraced by my tears,
Got a golden dress to wear,
Still felt like a priceless fire.
Got to held down,
A mountain brimming with anger,
Known by far through regret.
Fought with a dashing sword,
Ultimately got hooked up in the war.
Lit by the fire of anguish,
Shone by the beauty of humbleness,
Wished to get sway at night,
Rose up as lion in a day.
Ignited with the greed to get the crown,
At the same time, there is a fear of getting drowned.
Though hastiness makes my decision worn out,
Guiltless I am! Fair I was! A warrior myself!

9. THE SUPERHERO'S VILLAINY

They were once our superheroes
They used to be our protectors
But, now they have become the murderers!
The one, who is to halt the crime,
is now committing the crime!
Those heroes, who were supposed to fight like warriors against the evil,
Has now turned up as evil!
When we were harassed, we stood up in front of you.
But, now we clash against each other,
because, there is no ground to approach you,
as it turned out to be you, the one who seeded those.
Those guns which used to shoot down the culprit,
is now used against the guiltless.
The bullets you fling at us,
jabs at the back of our every bone.
The attire you wear, were once an untold story behind
Now, they became the told story of your misdeeds.
The batons which charged over to fight against the despotism,
is now used to slay two sinless lives?
They were flogged black and blue, with bruises,
which broke all your promises.
We are not heedless of the crisis,
but, we will all become the risers,
from this illicit, malicious tortures.

We will not be blinded anymore
We will raise our voice against your breach of the peace.
The trauma you caused them,
you have to be liable for their lives, one day.
The commotions you caused,
made your motions to be lost.
Once, you were the gem of our society to protect.
Now, you have become the germ to infect.
The blood they shed,
The abuse they endured,
The pain they tolerated,
The tears they shed,
The hunger they bear,
Everything needs to be equalised with your crimes being confessed,
And the punishment you receive, which torments you,
Shall remind you of the afflictions they underwent.

10. THE NOSY INTRUDERS

When I was locked up in a hooted jail,
I pictured the world through a veil
An insanity that got through my veins,
When I was undergoing a torturous pain.
My vision in a farsighted view,
Throwing a spontaneous beam of light.
The muddy smell of the murgeon,
Picked me up from my dreary dungeon.
I hid myself under a blanket,
For I wish not to see anymore.
My fingers were numb,
My legs were helpless.
When they accused me of the terror,
Which I know not.
My passion got diluted,
In a second of a fraction.
Those fingers that pointed at me,
Who historized my past,
Those mongers, vagabonds,
Not a thing to do in their lives
Who have the rights to intrude in my breath?
For I yearn to descry,
What the world has for me.
Though I despise it's mortals,

My fondness to leave no stone unturned,
Will always keep me like a cat on hot bricks.

PARTIALITY PHILTRE

11. MY ANGEL

Aw! That quieted lips, immaculate look,
Indolent walks, Ludicrous
Moves, Beguiling creature,
ever since you,
Stepped into my heart.
It Vanquish, it Deferral, it Loves, it
Aches
Know for what? ah!!!
only u? Mm, Nail me to your soul.
You made me shriek when I want to yowl,
You smirk when I'm disconsolate
Life can be holocaust but,
It is what that truly makes one strong.
Eternity slept away when I chat with you.
I cherish within my heart
Never imagined such a bliss happens,
Hope you know how much I care,
I'll always adore you.
Lost and alone, I'll no longer be,
Because you are here with me,
An angel is what you are to me.

12. A SPECIAL SOUL

In My Life Time,
I met a Special Soul,
He fills my very essence
it almost overflows,
I drink a cup of love and
It tastes like a ruby wine
And the day that we saw each other
filled with joy, happiness and shy
And You Know Within Your heart,
That Day Was Devine!!
No Distance Can Prevail.
An Inner Spark, Within the heart
the words that are spoken,
the emotions left unsaid,
the excitement i felt,
the way you made me smile,
the starting of a journey
in which we both shall be
a reflection of each other,
For All Eternity
never before had imagined
That Here On Earth
such A Bliss Could happen
Never Before
Until You!!!!!

13. THE BLISS IN NATURE

How elegant is the rain,
How nature has to gain,
The drops are like pearl falling down
the sky,
The surrounding seems to swirl high.
This day is cold, dark and dreary,
It rains and the wind is near weary.
The soil is forever soft.
Leaves unfold to hold each drop
Yeah! we had a most refreshing shower
which wetted all of us hearts,
All of a sudden, a wind blow
They let go, surprising you,
Sitting motionless under a Phoenix
tree.

14. THE MUSIC OF LIFE

Ah! I hear some noise which
tickles my mind & soul
I lend my ears but not of
myself,
having the mood to divert my
mind.
They still make me calm and
giving pleasure
I regret for being strange to
the familiar music
it's my heart beating in harmony a melody unique to
only me
It connects me with feelings
of all classes,
failures, heartbreaks, passion,
ears, friendship, strength &
love
Everything finds its new
beginning.
The music is fading again,
I love the music,
does it sound any better?

15. ARDENT FLAME

Does it exist? ETERNITY, the time without end?
Two flames bumping each other with destination,
Eternity, the time without end.
They bump, destined to encounter the destiny.
Can sea fled without sun? Knowest thou the shore,
where none of the breakers roar.
These flames whisper the confession of the night full of nothingness,
converse took flight as a complete stranger,
confide in each other as lifelong soul who is rare and red.
Aww! the fragrance of the flame;
bringing the weary soul to ease,
Eternity forever in heavenly breeze.
Two flames like two soul in the universe,
wondering about a thought of divine.
The grandeur lift the thought to things above;
Eternity is in sour.
Until the lengthening wax break into fire,
The contrarior moods of them recoil away.
Two flames deserved forever will posses the heart
which possess the soul indeed,
wishing to seize the state and the time after death;
and made the flame think of darkness in depth,
They stopped for a moment to encounter each other to love,
The two flames gazed upon the yonder shore;
And thus, undertook the journey to cross the sea together.

And here's a little parenthesis in eternity! fulfilled,
The crave to reach the Eternal home.

16. ETERNITY IN TIME

Two blended flames of love without resolution,
Bump, scrub, grasp and clasp,
Tread and tramp the infinity shores
Propping on the sea's clap
That echoes on the ears of Time
From sea to sun and moon to stars,
Filling nothingness to fullness.
Aww! the fragrance of the flame;
spiralling the weary soul to rise,
Stays in Heavenly breeze in the land of Time.
Forgetting the past, flinging the future
Merely residing in the boundless present
unscathed and unaffected.
Eternity of Eternities -
the end meets the beginning, the circle of unlimited space,
The spark of life inside Time - the Present,
The immovable posture; where moments are infinite,
Unceasing are memories, boundless is joy - the persistent accession.
The two soul flames,
whirling and dancing into oneness,
Attained eternity inside Time,
The Eternal home.

17. STRUGGLE OF YOUTH

O youth, youth, youth!
God! that golden time, I'm strong in truth,
To wear our heart and nerves and brain,
And give oneself a world of pain,
And quite are sinking with the strain.
Well, say you the world is a chamber of sleep
And life but a sleeping and dreaming?
But all if the world is a beautiful wild.
where struggle the weak with the stronger,
Then need no storm and no wife and no child!
They fight for the perishing future;
But, they stuck, they can die on the field.
Unable to run away, one is consumed with pain.
The decent into darkness was broken,
Revealing there is no I.
O, it's not joys and it's not bliss,
Only it is precisely this,
That keeps us still alive

18. BREAKING THE STIGMA

Hey, you'll, how are you?
lol. I am super fine! with a beautiful smirk.
I'm not lying said to me and myself.
how's me then? bit conquering my brain.
Found something like Broken. Rejected.
Betrayed. Defeated my heart whispered.
Amoniocentsis just to know,
Each huge division we watch as they grow.
Hear me! and stop lying.my heart.
A few commit crimes to be removed from pain
The stress and pressure to sprint consuming.
Keep silent I yelled to him.
Emotion dragging me and hit deeper.
To the barrenness of despair.
Looking into the shinning blistering sun
and warming my soul!
You'll I understood we all live with it.
And said as Craziness. Derangement. Lunacy.
Insaness, Madness, Mental disorder,
and yes. It's Psychopathy.
Bravely break it hard, Break the stigma.
I can survive by striking.
It's ok I'm always fine.

THE MEMORIES OF LITTLE WOUNDS

19. A POINTLESS CHASE

Can somebody teach me,
How is life supposed to be?
Is it merely a soft-swift ride,
Where we dwell with one sheer pride?
I see a heap!-
still a plenty to seek;
But It's fleeting ! ,
I suppose, I can't be meak.
Yet, Left with thousand problems to reflect;
Burdened to move with utmost circumspect.
Where do I start and where do I End!
With all these Endless questions to tend.
In a world of silence and sullen dark,
It's almost absurd to find my mark;
Is it fair, to endure this chaos for lifelong?
When I'm mad-vague about where I belong.
To grow, To cease and then to die!
Is this a modern theory , life imply!
If this is how, the journey, supposed to be-
Then, let us rest and savor the present glee!

20. TO THE MOON

The Moon that shines all night,
Well praised by millions for its light,
Little do we know the actual affairs,
For real, who holds the hopeless despairs.
All we see, is the grandeur Opulence;
But God knows who's with all due reverence.
In the wide ocean of countless stars,
How utterly friendless ,she might be around!
And all the loneliest wounds she scars,
Forsakes, craters on her forlorn ground!
The Pits and the dents endured for ages,
Greatly whacking, the patterns of her images;
Miserable thing! with these harrowing insecurities,
Striving to prove her sedulous self to her own arbitraries!
Does she know, we hail her from the below?
For the eyeful charm, observed through those billow!
Will she ever see herself, as Precious,
As a poem, penned by a Poet, gushes!

21. AMPHIGORY

How It all started will always remain a history,
And the way it still bothers me is arguably a mystery,
I'm good at letting my memories fade,
But this returns as a ball thrown at a Palisade.
Everytime I cogitate about this backstory,
I end up scribbling an amphigory.
Probably an unfinished business,
That We were unnerved to progress.
Or Perhaps, the hopeless me, felt us alike,
As a last leaf sticking to the rampike.
One true bond Ive had in a while ,
Which in my darkest days, made me smile.
God knows what fettered the souls that are not meant to be,
To get tangled up in a tragic turmoil that I can't outsee.
Years have passed, making troublers out of toddlers,
And Never once Have I been ungrateful, For the Time and trust ,which was blitheful.
Though I shackled the promises I proposed,
I'm Unapologetic for the hurt I imposed,
Cause I had known it's just a passing hue,
Which I hoped to subside without a clue.
Helpless but with constant dilemmas-
I had to face while watching my favourite cinemas.
I pondered to get a fix on that.
only to discover a fruitless reverie, in fact.

Nevertheless, You'll always be remembered ,
In the column of ill-choises.
A lost cause,
In my secret diary of great loss.
And I'll always Hope you're with the one, fittingly deserving for you.
But again, It's a lie, if I say it hurts not,
to see you with someone new.

22. NATURE - A HAVEN FOR HUMAN

Things are deformed - Now
that we hail the terraformed,
The flying engine that transits,
And the droid that counterfeits,
All Has Marked, a new normal
For the nonce;
Now that we've deposed the designer,
From the ghetto of the Far-flung celestials;
I could clearly see the breakthrough we pined for,
But the gaiety and tranquility,
is nowhere near, to what we hoped for;
In this mercurial war, that vacillates,
I can vividly presage the days, ahead in time-
A time ,When peace and pleasure, becomes a 'lost cause';
The hollow humans, would snapback,
To the woods, they wrecked in the erstwhile;
When the devised turmoil, destroys our last hope-
The mortal mobs might rebound
To the once neglected Nature
And the generous Greens that were betrayed
Would help the ungrateful hunters yet again!
Doomed by the clouded and the gloomy skies,
It's Nature that snuffs them out From the tartarus fright!
And a small streak of it's mighty light,

Would instill in heart, a sanguine sight !

23. MY FAIRY GRANDMOTHER

Way beyond the misty weather,
On teeth trembling day of the winter
With her beloved, beaten up bag,
Hanging down her wrinkled wrist;
She Dolls me up, with the best dress on!
And sets an hour of absolute wonderment,
She takes me down the bustling street,
Holding me on her worn out waist-
Even amidst the intense bargain brawls,
She keeps me in hold, with her caring grip,
With the Little money rolled-up in her shrink bag,
She Spends on me till her heart gets pleased;
With the savings treasured, just for the cause-
She Gets me goodies, I wouldn't even ask for!
But Life is Cruel and So is the time,
That hits us when we least prepare
My fairy God-Grandmother she was!
To Whom, I harken back only in photographs!

24. SOCIAL STIGMAS MUSINGS OF A MAIDEN

Let's not forget that day -
When we were happy and not at dismay,
Away from all these burdens-
that rack up, as we become maidens.
It's now, gone for good and forever,
With the stolen bliss, we might never recover.
But those non-chalant juvenile days,
Hooked In our dim memories, still stays.
Deemed as affronts for being radical in reality-
Though they ace in books that talk Equality.
Stigmatized with sniding names they perceived
Only by the petty patterns they had conceived!
So Tell me,
How could we ever feel pampered,
If the freedom we yearn for, is being hindered ?

25. THE BEAUTIFUL BANE

All my bootless merry chase, portray-
My hopes to ride on clouds, some day;
Turns out, nowt but a senseless stay,
A mad woman, Stumbling to choose her way!
And, At far, I see a bright, big door;
Seducing my steps to seek for more,
This bad call, urged my itch to soar,
The evil, disguised in an innocent sore.
Not all that shines are really gold,
Scary things are oft not told,
Only by ordeals,do we see the fouled?
A desideratum, vital yet unviable to withhold!
Thwart thyself from this beautiful bane,
Everytime you sense of losing your sane,
By and by, you'll hear the sirens to wane ,
A note to be preserved, in the memory lane.

26. THE SHE IN ME

She's pretty, She's Potent,
She's more than what they judge.
She's smart, She's stubborn,
She's raring to get the un-getable
She's all alone, but
She never needed one.
She fails on her strife, but
She never retires.
She's still miles away- But
She's unstoppable.
She's tired as hell, but
She'll never be lazy.
She has her dreams and
She'll never go easy.
She's disdained everyday, but
She's far ahead of their dogmas;
Thanks to her Cause-
That causes her to fight,
All Braced up and Balanced,
Up until the upshot -
When her frisky self, Needs
No-one else to preach her cachet.

27. MOVING THROUGH THE STILL TIME

I Started out as a child,
Whining to grow a little too sooner,
Wondering how it feels
To be tall and unafraid; To lock and unlock-
The tall doors of our abode.
To look beyond the crowds, without
Being held up by a hand.
To let others swing to and fro
In the iron like fire arms- That
my father shows off as some secret forte.
I had no idea,
That it takes yonks to grow up!
Somehow, I chased it.
And here I'm, As an adult!
Which feels nothing like the child I was!

The hustle and bustle I'm expected to cope with,
Loosing the true me for some loaves of bread;
To fake a personality to fit in this society,
This Ain't nothing like the adulthood
I had in my mind!
Twenty Two and stuck in this society,
I've lost my interest in this insanity!
If only had I had a time machine,

I would perhaps go back in years,
Moving through the still time,
To meet the child I was, And remind her,
How precious childhood is!

28. THE METAMORPHOSIS

Solely an arrant gaiety -
Ever since she espied this debased ferity;
The notions of her rapturous agility,
Blinded her from the repulsive reality.
Little did she know, she's a girl,
Born to become a woman with sanity -
In this guild of geezers and teasers,
To become a pleaser to the seekers ;
Toing and froing with her chums
In the far end swing,
Fighting like cats and dogs for their
Turn before the ring.
Every day felt like a fairy tale,
Only Until she sauntered back to her abode,
An unnamed hunch filled the gale -
As many gazed at her as she strode.
They Muttered and tittered all her way,
But no one nerved to explain the dismay,
Meanwhile, Her nonchalant self,
Didn't care to bounce airily till her doors,
She hugged her mom, saying
'Here I come ! Your little one',
Mom, descried her stains and said,
'No darling, not anymore'.

29. THE DEVOID PRESENCE

Blue are blurred by the
Blatant lies you blandish,
Pinks or pissed off as
A price of my ignorance,
Greens grew gothic for the
Grave concern I had for you,
Violets became voided without
Your vehement touch of love,
Blacks are getting blooded from
Bemoaning your absence,
Oranges ostracize you now, for
They miss the old you,
Whites are whining for the
'We', we hoped for,
And yellows are yearning
For you to come back.
All colors crave you,
Despite the nothingness,
You left us for.
It's always colorless,
In this cursed meadow -
A world where you're still,
But Devoid !

9 798887 837352

Printed by Libri Plureos GmbH in Hamburg, Germany